Yor Anne + Stephen —
I hope you enjoy this
of poetry. Your painting on the
cover of my book is the perfect
reflection of who I am today.

A RIVER OF HOPE

BOOK OF POETRY

RIVER MICHAELS

Wishing you both much love,
peace & happiness

River Michaels

you are
beautiful

The opinions expressed in this manuscript are solely the opinions of the author and do not represent the opinions or thoughts of the publisher. The author represents and warrants that she either owns or has the legal right to publish all material in this book.

A River of Hope – Book of Poetry
All Rights Reserved.
Copyright © 2017 River Michaels
V1.0

Cover Photo Credit: Laura R. Michaels, Painting by Lori Anne Boocks©
All photos are copyright to the individual photographer as indicated in this book.

This book may not be reproduced, transmitted, or stored in whole or in part by any means, including graphic, electronic, or mechanical without the express written consent of the publisher except in the case of brief quotations embodied in critical articles and reviews.

Lulu Press, Inc.
Morrisville, North Carolina
http://www.lulu.com

ISBN: 978-1-387-21010-7

PRINTED IN THE UNITED STATES OF AMERICA

FOREWORD

It's a rare joy to read something that truly inspires you. Not surprisingly, River Michaels has this ability, because "inspiring" and "joyful" are at the top of the list of words I would use to describe her as a person. River has a reverence and deep empathy for humanity that shine through in her poetry. *A River of Hope* takes you on a relatable journey, from beginning to end, you feel as though you are on this ride with a close friend. Complex feelings are given clarity with such ease that you know your author is truly gifted. This poetry journey is one with a magnificent view and the selected artwork/photographs are astounding and tells a story of their own. It is a moving journey of the heart that feels as though it was thoughtfully planned for you alone.

River Michaels is the real thing! She is genuine, her poetry taps into profound, painful and even devastating topics while leaving us encouraged, happy and optimistic. River's poetry comes from a very personal place; however, it is universal – I feel as though she is writing from my life experiences. When I read River's poems, I think about them often; I return again and again only to find deeper meaning.

Thank you for sharing your extraordinary gift!

Barbara A. Tatum, M.B.A.
Wichita State University, Kansas
Professional Academy of Health Care Management

PREFACE

A River of Hope - Book of Poetry is a collection of poems that express my life experiences and reflect who I am at the age of fifty as an American Poet. We are all born with our unique talents and mine is condensing a story, a message, or a reflection of the times all neatly wrapped in a five-stanza poem.

My poetry is primarily about the fleeting nature of time and tender matters of the heart. Like a song that can immediately transport you to a place in time, the same is true for me with each of my poems. The beauty of poetry is that it speaks to each person differently based on their frame of reference or state of mind.

It has been my experience that the most thoughtful gifts are those that come from the heart. If a poem in this book was written in the spirit of you, then you have left an eternal heart print on my soul.

Love and Peace,

River Michaels

DEDICATION

I would like to dedicate, *A River of Hope - Book of Poetry*, to the victims of Hurricane Harvey. On Saturday, August 26, 2017, Hurricane Harvey, a Category 4 hurricane made landfall at peak intensity at Rockport, Texas with winds of 130 mph. The storm made a second landfall in Texas as a Category 3 hurricane. Afterwards, rapid weakening ensued as its speed slowed dramatically to a crawl, and weakened to a tropical storm. For the next two days, the storm stalled just inland over the Houston area dropping very heavy rainfall and causing widespread catastrophic flash flooding. On Tuesday, August 29, 2017, the storm continued east over the Beaumont/Port Arthur area causing devastating flooding, water supplies were cut off, and chemical plants were exploding in Crosby, Texas. Ultimately, the Texas and Louisiana Gulf coasts suffered extreme damage and loss of life.

On a personal note, my sister's house was one of the thousands of homes flooded in the Houston area and my extended family in Mauriceville, TX. The spirit of Texas is that of immense love, support, pain, and sacrifice as they rebuild their homes and communities. I firmly believe that they will be better, stronger, and more hopeful than before. The outpouring of support from neighbors, volunteers, and fundraising efforts of so many celebrities that have contributed to help save the victims and animals affected by the storm is tremendous and exceptional.

May God bless all the people affected not only by Hurricane Harvey, but also from Hurricane Irma and Hurricane Maria that have devastated Florida, Cuba, Virgin Islands, Barbuda, Puerto Rico, and the Dominican Republic. My heart goes out to the families that lost everything, including their loved ones.

TABLE OF CONTENTS

FOREWORD .... **III**

PREFACE .... **IV**

DEDICATION .... **V**

INTRODUCTION **1**

INSPIRATION **3**

Makes My Soul Sing 6
The Universe 8
Yesterday's Rose 10
Wear the Crown 12
Points to the North 14
A Thread in Life's Weave 16
You Believe 18
The White Bear 20

SORROW AND HEARTACHE **21**

Carson Cade Broussard 23
The Sad True Happiness 24
Piano Man 26
Seattle Rain 28
My Daughter, My Mother 30
Without Their Love 32
I Am Living Out Loud 34
Rumination Road 36
These Words 38
This I Know for Sure 40

RECOVERY **41**

Into the Wind 44
Days of Blue 46
Face Your Fear 48
One Grain at a Time 50
Waltzing Through My Dream 52
A Place Called Home 54

After the Rain 56

GRATITUDE   57

A Runaway Horse 60

One Breath Away 62

In Our Creator's Eye 64

Learn to Forgive 66

Sowing the Seeds 68

What You Already Have 70

THE TIMES   71

Aligning the Stars 74

Lost Their Pulse 76

The Angelic Voice 78

Love in Your Voice 80

Wake of an Eagle 82

Strike of a Spark 84

LOVE   85

This Road that She Paved 88

Standing in the Middle 90

The Look in Their Eye 92

Light the Stars 94

Away from the Shore 96

I Knew It Was You 98

SELF-REFLECTION   99

Among the Stars 102

A Different Sea 104

Same River Twice 106

Both Young and Old 108

I Am River 110

ABOUT THE AUTHOR   111

I AM 112

OTHER BOOKS BY RIVER MICHAELS   113

INTRODUCTION

At the age of fifty, I think of my mother and the pearls of wisdom she passed down to me. My mother lived on this earth for sixty-one years, 1 month and 29 days. I remember the day when Mom turned fifty. We were living together in Valley Lee, Maryland while I was in the Navy stationed at Naval Air Station Patuxent River, Maryland. We were renting an old small house split as a duplex on a small piece of land walking distance to the Chesapeake Bay. I took a picture of her standing in front of a tree in our yard. I have kept that photograph near me all these years, and now as I look at it, I realize how young and beautiful she was at the time.

I have learned that it is best to always remember the good in people instead of the glaring mistakes we have all made during our lives. I honestly have only good memories of my mother. She was my best and true friend. There were several people over the years that would dominate my life while she was still alive but in the end, my mother always came first. It is interesting to realize how stubborn and naïve we are in our youth even though the answer is staring us in the face. My mother always called it as she saw it, and she was invariably right about the people and choices I made. Wisdom comes with age and experience as I now rethink my choices and strive to become a better, kinder, gentler, environmentally conscious, animal loving person. My mother is the voice in my head when I am upset, when I am happy, and when I am about to make a life-changing decision. For all that is good inside of me is directly attributed to her loving guidance and unconditional love.

It is my mother's thoughts, words, proverbs, and expressions I would like to share with my readers as I believe them to be helpful to anyone struggling through the obstacles of life.

- If it's not yours, leave it alone.
- If you do not want a secret to be repeated, do not tell another soul.
- Do your best today and tomorrow will take of itself.
- Nothing stays the same; this too shall pass.
- Only focus on the things you can control, if it is not in your control, let it go.
- What happens in the dark, will always come to light.
- When you make a mistake, acknowledge it, accept it, because when you know better, strive to do better.
- Be kind to people, you never know what they are going through, and a simple smile can light a string around their heart.
- No matter how bad you think you have it, someone else has it much worse. Find gratitude in all that you have.
- Always have something to look forward to each day.
- Embrace your hobbies and don't over-think things.
- Break down big ideas into small, doable pieces and take life one day at a time.
- Know that music is healing and transformative.
- Take the time to appreciate the beauty of a tree, a flower, and a vista.
- Acknowledge the beauty in yourself today; you may not realize how beautiful you have always been until an old photograph emerges.
- Don't believe everything you see, after all, sugar looks a lot like salt.
- Know there is much more to life than meets the eye.

May you find peace, joy, love, hope, and inspiration in the following collection of my poetry.

INSPIRATION

"You are a child of the universe, no less than the trees and the stars; you have a right to be here. And whether or not it is clear to you, no doubt the universe is unfolding as it should. Therefore, be at peace with God, whatever you conceive Him to be, and whatever your labors and aspirations, in the noisy confusion of life keep peace with your soul. With all its shams, drudgery, and broken dreams, it is still a beautiful world. Be cheerful. Strive to be happy."
~ Max Ehrmann 1927 Desiderata©

Photo credit: Laura R. Michaels © 2017

The "HOU DAT" on my T-shirt represents the city of Houston and New Orleans united in the wake of Hurricane Harvey. This shirt was made by Fleurty Girl in New Orleans, Louisiana and all proceeds went to help the victims of Hurricane Harvey in September 2017. For more information, please visit their website:
www.fleurtygirl.net

MAKES MY SOUL SING

In the middle of the night, down came the rain,
With so much water and no place to drain...
We raised our belongings as high as we could,
But the water kept rising as we knew it would...

Look out the window, it's hard to believe,
Our neighborhoods have now become a sea...
The wildlife is swimming in the raging river,
They too, have nowhere to go and are left to shiver...

There are blinking lights in hopes to be seen,
Of those trapped in their homes trying to scream...
A couple is rescued, but their baby swept away,
These raging waters have stolen their prey...

An officer drowns while doing his best,
Everyone mourns as he is laid to rest...
The sun appeared at the end of the day,
As a symbol of hope, now we pray...

With tears of joy to see the sun,
We will rebuild our lives one by one...
Our hands join together as a united ring,
This outpouring of love *Makes My Soul Sing*...

"They say a person needs just three things to be truly happy in this world: someone to love, something to do, and something to hope for."
~ T. Bodett

THE UNIVERSE

When we emit a vibration into the universe,
It will come back like the wings that flap in reverse...
This energy will hover and sit with our heart,
Just like old friends that were never apart...

Sometimes you're the bird and others the feeder,
When you have lost your hope, search for the leader...
There are highs and lows of the weak and strong,
Remember the source is love and where you belong...

They say when the student is ready, the teacher appears,
And low and behold, it has brought you right here...
Be open to love and what you need to learn,
Turn your fears into tinder and watch them burn...

There is a symphony of notes that beg you to sing,
Like the joy of a child that flies in the swing...
Similarities attract and then flows in accord,
And you will never be as you were before...

Like a playful silliness that makes you giggle,
To remind you of love as you stand in the middle...
When the hummingbird appears and flaps in reverse,
Know it is your sign of love from *The Universe*...

Photo Credit: Lois Evelyn McCauley © 1944
In Photo: My Mother

YESTERDAY'S ROSE

Our thoughts become energy that manifest in time,
They create the reality between yours and mine…
We tend to borrow our thoughts from yesterday,
Crowding the space in a brand new day…

All living things must learn to cope,
Everything around is bursting with hope…
Like a tiny seedling to a blade of grass,
Or spinning sand that turns to glass…

Find peace and joy in the simplest things,
Like the beautiful bird with the speedy wings…
What *God* said to the rose that made her bloom,
He said to your heart as it grew in the womb…

As you lie awake at night in your bed,
May loving thoughts run through your head…
Like puppy dog breath and their sleepy eyes,
And their little licks when you cry…

I see the light in your soul that is full of grace,
And the pool in your eyes is a magical place…
Find peace in your heart before it goes,
Like the pedals that fall from *Yesterday's Rose*…

Photo credit: Vanya Willoughby © 2015
In Photo: (left to right) Laura R. Michaels, Patty Canastra-Heenan, Mary Gentry, Beth Crimmins, and River Michaels "Carpe Diem Ladies"

Patty "Hot Lips" Canastra-Heenan is an extraordinary woman that continues to inspire me every day. She is the most ambitious woman I have ever met. I met Patty while running a 5K in Fairfax, Virginia in May 2014. Since then, Patty and I ran a biathlon, the Army 10 Miler at the Pentagon, the Marine Corp Marathon 10k that begins at the Pentagon and ends at the Iwo Jima Memorial in Arlington, Virginia.

A group of us, aptly named *"Carpe Diem Ladies,"* include Beth "Dusty" Crimmins, Mary "Dot" Gentry, Vanya Willoughby (not shown), and Laura "Dash" Michaels. We even traveled to Dublin, Ireland in August 2015 to run the *Rock & Roll Half-Marathon* through the city and parks of Dublin. Our last run together (to date) was at Yellowstone National Park in June 2016. These ladies continue to inspire me and always will!

WEAR THE CROWN

When we decide to start something new,
Some will bite off more than they can chew…
Most will leap and make giant strides,
And some will gently roll with the tide…

We move along at a steady pace,
Just keep going and finish the race…
People will pass as if you're standing still,
But you will see them again at the top of the hill…

You must dig deep and tap into the source,
There are many metaphors while running the course…
Only you can control your endurance and thoughts,
Visualize a map in your mind and connect the dots…

Most problems will occur in the first part of the run,
You may be tempted to quit when it's no longer fun…
But you will always find that if you proceed,
You will find a way to pick up speed…

It is very satisfying to have a goal,
It gives you a reason to take control…
Without a challenge, we're drifting around,
So, make it happen and *Wear the Crown*…

Photo Credit: Laura R. Michaels © 2017

POINTS TO THE NORTH

Some days move seemingly fast,
What is alive today will soon be the past…
This speeding pendulum we call time,
The older we get, the louder it chimes…

You have your routine day in and day out,
Like an absent person who's walking about…
You may never know when somebody cares,
As you stand in the mirror, lost in a stare…

It's the rooted soul that seeps in your eyes,
And the laugh or two that keeps your disguise…
The perceptive one sees the gap in your heart,
That delicate place where the shadows part…

When you close your eyes in a meditative state,
Find the charm in serendipity and timeless fate…
When you can release misère and all its pain,
There is peace that flows in the pouring rain…

All of your experiences are now understood,
Always believe that you did the best you could…
Keep your back to the wind and always go forth,
And follow the star that *Points to the North*…

Photo Credit: Laura R. Michaels © 2017

A THREAD IN LIFE'S WEAVE

There is a cyclical nature throughout time,
When one light dims, another will shine…
We each are responsible for extending a hand,
When someone has fallen, help them to stand…

In the muddy waters, we are stepping blind,
But you never know what you may find…
When life deals you a blow into your chest,
Always remember that you are blessed…

Nothing feels better than being kind,
A thoughtful gesture pleases the mind…
When you help someone else, you will feel better,
Send them a note, a card, or an old fashion letter…

Always remember that this too shall pass,
Yesterday's shadow will live in the past …
Here comes the rainbow of many colors,
What you bring to the world is like no other…

You may never know how beautiful you are,
Or the healing peace you have on a scar…
But none of that matters when you believe,
That we are simply *A Thread in Life's Weave*…

Photo Credit: Alex A. Benten © 2001

This was my last birthday with my mother. This hug means so much to me. These are my final gifts from her. When she signed my birthday card, she wrote:

"You are strong, and you'll be strong... I love you, Mams"

YOU BELIEVE

It's evening time in the nursing ward,
Shifts are changing, and the lonely are bored…
Patients arrive in their worst possible state,
With no desire to eat, they stare at their plate…

There is no rest for the tired and weak,
Lying in their gowns never wanting to speak…
Looking around the room with hopeful eyes,
For someone to see them through their disguise…

The agony of being trapped in a ragged frame,
Feeling invisible in life and pulled from the game…
Some will live for their families, but others don't,
Some will live for love, but others won't…

But time is a continuum with so many layers,
And our simplest needs are filled by prayer…
Happiness will not reside in money or greed,
It lives in the life that grows from a seed…

So, here's to the nurses that make their rounds,
May they recognize even the slightest of sounds…
For they are the ones that will tend to your needs,
And squeeze your hand so that *You Believe*…

"You best teacher is your last mistake."
~ Buddha

THE WHITE BEAR

Who do you see when you look in the mirror?
Look into your eyes and the image is clearer…
We are not our bodies as it would seem,
We are intelligent dust floating in a dream…

We will always obsess over what we try to avoid,
These mental games were analyzed by Freud…
You convince yourself that you do not care,
Think of whatever you want - just not the white bear…

You let the white bear cut you so many times,
It punctures so deep that it's hard to climb…
But hand over fist you can rise again,
With a protected soul and a stronger chin…

You can decide to turn the page,
But to measure the distance is hard to gauge…
Keep your eyes to the sun and don't look back,
Tighten your rope and get rid of the slack…

If you have a white bear that haunts your mind,
Just shine your light until he is blind…
You can convince yourself not to live in despair,
And think of whatever you want - even *The White Bear*…

SORROW AND HEARTACHE

"One always dies too soon - or too late. Yet, one's whole life is complete at that moment, with a line drawn neatly under it, ready for the summing up. You are - your life, and nothing else."
~ J. P. Sartre

CARSON CADE BROUSSARD

Carson Cade Broussard was born on July 25, 1996, and a native of Houston TX and resident of Katy, TX. Carson passed away at 6:55 am on Saturday, December 21, 2013, at Texas Children's Hospital in Houston. He was 17 years old.

Carson was a junior at Cinco Ranch High School where he was a member of the football and wrestling team before his illness. His analytical mind earned him a place in the gifted and talented program. A bright student, he also excelled at Chess. He was a talented musician who played drums and piano. Carson was diagnosed in September 2012 with Leukemia. His determination and courage inspired his mother, peers, caregivers, and most of all, his entire family. Carson's zest for life touched many people and will leave behind a legacy that will never be forgotten.

The last book that Carson read was *"Fault in Our Stars,"* and the last poem he wrote was *"The Sad True Happiness."*

THE SAD TRUE HAPPINESS

In my own world, I lay watching the youth,
sadness, happiness, life, and death all fade
becoming the ultimate mundane truth.
There is no purpose for which we are made.
Set aside altruistic behavior.
For upon death it is all meaningless.
Do exactly as you desire.
You have but one brief, inane existence.
Find the sad true happiness,
or find the secret to immortality.
Carson Broussard
~ Forever 17

Painting and Photo Credit: River Michaels © 2014

Photo Credit: Rachael Broussard ©

I wrote the poem, *"Piano Man,"* on the day that Carson passed away and read it aloud at his funeral in front of his family and friends. It was an unforgettable moment in my life that forever changed who I am. He was a bright star that dimmed much too soon. For those that knew him, and the loving spirit of his family, are forever blessed. Carson, we will all see you again one day when we meet you on the other side. Cheers to the young man that beat everyone in *Guitar Hero* ® with his perfect scores, I hope you are rockin' away in Heaven! Carson, you are so loved and missed.

PIANO MAN

This young soul touched so many lives,
For so many nights he fought to survive…
The endless needles and intravenous bags,
It all ceased today when he raised the white flag…

He died on the longest night of the year,
A winter solstice filled with sorrow and fear…
His mother's chest now burns with a hollow pain,
As his material items are all that remain…

There is comfort in knowing that his wings have spread,
And he was freed from the body that lay on the bed…
Just remember his voice and the warmth of his smile,
He is finally at peace and can rest for a while…

Know that in time your pain will subside,
But it won't be tonight so go ahead and cry…
Feel the anger inside and shout to the sky,
For, in the end, only *God* knows why…

But this young man did not die in vain,
He will live in the sunshine and the falling rain…
Yes, this *Piano Man* is playing in the heavens above,
He is the silence between the notes that are filled with love…

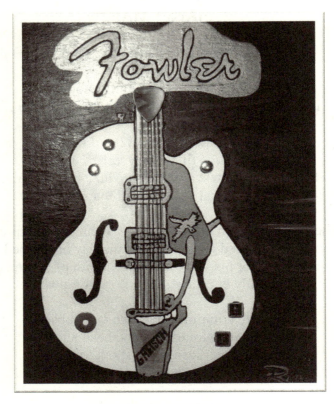

Painting and Photo Credit: River Michaels © 2015

I wrote the poem, *"Seattle Rain,"* for Timothy Mark Fowler of Seattle, Washington, who lost his battle with pancreatic cancer on October 18, 2015. I am grateful that he read this poem before he passed. He was 48 years old.

SEATTLE RAIN

I've been strong all my life, but now I am weak,
Treating this cancer feels like it's killing me…
I wish I could run, but I can't even walk,
In and out of my mind it's so hard to talk…

I miss my guitars and how they healed the gloom,
But now they stand at attention in their room…
They each have a voice that is all their own,
How I long for the sound of their beautiful tones…

My dear sweet friends don't know what to say,
The time passes slowly as I cling to this day…
As the orderly pushed and wheeled me inside,
I felt the sun on my face, and I wanted to cry…

I've lost so much weight that I don't know who I am,
What was once so important, now I don't give a damn…
I think about my greatest love and what that means,
I have been loved very deeply, and now I see…

I don't know what will happen but come what may,
You stay on my mind in the light of day…
I pray for a time when I'm no longer in pain,
If I could only survive this *Seattle Rain*....

I wrote the poem, *"My Daughter, My Mother,"* in loving memory of my aunt, Annette Rissenger, who lost her battle with cancer on February 14, 2014.

MY DAUGHTER, MY MOTHER

When a mother learns that her child is a girl,
That's when she knows she has a friend in this world...
There's a special bond between a daughter and a mother,
It's different from a father, a son or even a brother...

When a mother's daughter becomes an adult,
They hope for a friendship in which to consult...
Even when they fight and often disagree,
A reflection in the mirror is what they see...

When daylight comes, and her mind isn't there,
The daughter will wash and comb her hair...
That gentle caress will touch her soul,
Without a word, it's her hand that you hold...

When all is exhausted in her care,
The daughter can whisper a silent prayer...
It is a mother's love that runs through your veins,
When her physical body no longer remains...

As the corrosive nature of time takes her away,
She will live inside you for the rest of your days...
There is a circle of life from one to the other,
An everlasting love - *My Daughter, My Mother*...

"Where there is love, there is pain."
~ Spanish Proverb

WITHOUT THEIR LOVE

When someone dies that you love inside,
Their loving touch haunts your mind...
When your heart is aching in so much grief,
Down on your knees begging for relief...

When the night is over, and the dawn is near,
Open your eyes and say hello to fear...
To start another day without a direction,
Searching all day for that lost affection...

Time is ticking, and your heart keeps beating,
These daunting thoughts are all but fleeting...
Then the day comes to pack up the past,
Deciding what to keep and what will last...

Each step you take is like wet cement,
If you idle too long, you will start to resent...
As painful as it is to experience this loss,
It is the price of love, no matter the cost...

Every journey begins with a single step,
Now pick up the pieces with all that's left...
Believe that they are with you from above,
Where would you be *Without Their Love*...?

Photo Credit: River Michaels © 1999

In loving memory of the kindest, smartest, warmest, and most loving woman I have ever known, my mother:

Laurel Candace Guice

July 7, 1940 – September 5, 2001

I AM LIVING OUT LOUD

I will never forget the day when my mom sat me down,
She had something to tell me, and her face had a frown…
She said she has cancer; it is now in stage four,
She was given a year of life but not much more…

My mind could not conceive of the words that she said,
How could I live if my mother was dead…?
She said "I feel fine and tomorrow has no guarantee,"
More than herself, she was worried about me…

Of course, I fell apart and down to my knees,
My biggest fear is now staring back at me…
First came the surgery and then recovery,
Get ready for chemo - rounds one, two and three…

An experimental drug bought her more time,
But the inevitable came with all its signs…
On a September morning, she gave her last breath,
I cried and cried until there was nothing left…

I had never planned to live without her,
But the days on the calendar became a blur…
Then I decided to live my life to make her proud,
That's why you feel me now, *I Am Living Out Loud*…

"Sometimes you can't let go of what's making you sad, because it was the only thing that made you happy..."
~ Anonymous

RUMINATION ROAD

We play these scenarios over again,
Somehow believing that we can rewrite the end...
But the silence will echo more than a sound,
And send us on a journey towards the lost and found...

We all have a choice to choose the right thing,
And we each are responsible for the energy we bring...
We can procrastinate the inevitable and cause a delay,
Or think before we speak the words that we say....

Yet we cry and moan just once more,
Then we wipe our eyes but leave a foot in the door...
The morning comes, and we want to feel better,
But how many times can we reread that letter...?

So, let's do some exercise and eat healthy food,
And not look away when we see ourselves nude,
Let's take a deep breath and lift our head to the sky,
And stand a little taller and stop asking why...

Finally - the moment arrives, and we're feeling strong,
And we found the courage to press play on that song...
But damn the warm blood that begins to run cold,
Now here we go again down *Rumination Road*...

"The secret of health for both mind and body is not to mourn for the past, worry about the future, or anticipate troubles but to live in the present moment wisely and earnestly."
~ Buddha

THESE WORDS

These words are rattling inside of my heart,
Echoing the silence of memories tearing apart…
These faithful chambers are bound to burst,
These letters are spelling words of hurt…

These words are seeping into my veins,
Searching for crevices to fill with pain…
My thoughts are words that haunt my mind,
Infecting the peace and stealing my time…

These words are the fabric of my cells,
Stinging my heart and crashing the bells…
Random surges of panic are fluttering about,
Reminders of what I can't do without…

These words need thoughts to fuel their power,
Turning seconds into minutes that fill the hours…
But imaginary locks can control the flow,
You light the words that you want to glow…

These words are equivocal in the good and bad,
They can make you happy or make you sad…
You choose the font, the weight, and how they burn,
Your letters are dancers that become *These Words*…

"As she has planted, so does she harvest; such is the field of karma."
~ Sri Guru Granth Sahib

THIS I KNOW FOR SURE

When a temptation arises that we know is wrong,
Do not strum the string that plays that song…
When your mind is addicted to the erotic thrill,
Who pays the price and whose blood will spill…?

This lure and seduction that feeds you internally,
Convincing you into a false sense of security…
Deceitful intentions are like poison arrows,
It destroys the life of an innocent sparrow…

If you think you're an actor ready for the part,
Is there another's life that will be torn apart?
Passion is temporary and possesses the mind,
Your words and actions will never rewind…

If history repeats and you don't know why,
Listen to your thoughts before it all goes awry…
When faced with a choice, ask these two questions,
Will this move me forward? Or, will this cause regression…?

Sometimes moving forward is a drive off a cliff,
Is your conscious clear without any ifs…?
Are you selfish because the pain is not yours?
What goes around comes around, *This I Know for Sure…*

RECOVERY

"There are things that we don't want to happen but have to accept, things we don't want to know but have to learn, and people we can't live without but have to let go."
~ Author Unknown

"In the end, only three things matter: how much you loved, how gently you lived, and how gracefully you let go of things not meant for you."
~ Buddha

INTO THE WIND

No one is the villain in their own play,
Some will never see the errors of their ways…
Troubled shadows can appear larger than life,
Projecting a reality filled with pain and strife…

We've all had these people in our lives,
The ones that cut you deep inside…
But there comes a time to sever the chord,
And you have to choose what to ignore…

These haunting memories will only churn,
But you have the choice not to let them burn…
A person in pain will rewrite the script,
Stoking the fire until it shifts…

We all have a need to protect the young,
And sometimes it's hard to hold your tongue…
Some lessons in life are more difficult than others,
And even more volatile when you're a mother…

Heal this wound now and let it go,
Let peace in your life and let it flow…
Let the anger inside come to an end,
And blow the hatred *Into the Wind*…

"Believe, when you are most unhappy, that there is something for you to do in the world. So long as you can sweeten another's pain, life is not in vain."
~ Helen Keller

DAYS OF BLUE

We all are responsible for the energy we bring,
We all have moods that are bound to swing…
But you never know whose day you'll make,
Just by showing up may ease their ache…

An ant, an owl, a fish or a tree,
We all need love and energy…
All living things have an equal heart,
We all have the purpose to play our part…

No two signatures are exactly the same,
Just as no two souls have identical flames…
Accept who you are and find peace within,
Let your burdens breathe and shed the skin…

The choice is yours to fill the glass,
Our physical lives are not meant to last…
The weight of the world is not your shoulders,
Each trip around the sun you're only getting older…

You can see falling debris or shooting stars,
You can hear a twang or a sweet guitar…
You can choose the light passes through,
And learn when to shield those *Days of Blue*…

"Time is a sort of river of passing events, and strong is its current; no sooner is a thing brought to sight than it is swept by and another takes its place, and this too will be swept away."
~ M. Aurelius

FACE YOUR FEAR

There is only one time when innocence is lost,
You can never go back when the line has been crossed...
Like the first night you drank and then sick till dawn,
You discovered the friends you could count on...

Your deepest love will be the one,
That hurt you the most and made you run...
You'll never forget how it felt to be punched,
These are the moments that happen once...

Your child will arrive only one time,
And they too will leave this world behind...
There is only one moment when you were born,
And you only die once leaving others to mourn...

Some things in life never happen twice,
Like the loss of a parent and you wail all night...
There is one time when you scream that primal cry,
When your loved one dies, and you're riddled with why???

Even with people around that have felt this pain,
There is no way to prepare for that oncoming train...
You will fall for the lies that you want to hear,
But you will love again when you *Face Your Fear*...

"You have not lived until you have done something for someone who can never repay you."
~ Anonymous

ONE GRAIN AT A TIME

All living beings share this same space in time,
There is no difference between what is yours and mine…
We all have a script that navigates our lives,
Be it destiny or fate - only you can decide…

Animals have a purpose with a mission of their own,
They see the world in a way that we've never known…
It was a greater design that created the wild,
When they too were born, their mother smiled…

Remember that everything is in a state of change,
What was familiar yesterday - may now feel strange…
We each are accountable for the words that we say,
Since life and death are born each day…

If your heart is still beating inside of your chest,
Then hope is alive so always do your best!
Like an electrical lyric that hums through your brain,
Charging the life in your spirit while the body remains…

Treasure the ones who travel by your side,
The elephant never forgets the one who's been kind…
So, focus on the goal but keep your mind on the climb,
Like the ant that builds the mound, *One Grain at a Time*…

"All that we see or seem, is but a dream within a dream."
~Edgar Allan Poe

WALTZING THROUGH MY DREAM

You came to see me just last night,
There was no sound or shining light…
Looking the same as when you were mine,
Preserved for me, this moment in time…

I've seen your face many times before,
And every time, you walked out the door …
You wandered through the garden of stones,
Your spirit transcended through my bones…

I felt so elated when I saw your face,
You've been gone so long and without a trace…
Your familiar eyes sparked a connection,
As I lay there reveling in your affection…

I don't know why I can't forget the past,
Perhaps it's because, I believed it would last…
I rewind the memories we recorded together,
When you used to love me, and promised forever…

But once again, you said farewell,
Waved your wand and cast the spell…
As you faded away, I could only scream,
As you kept on *Waltzing Through My Dream*…

Photo Credit: Brian Swank © 2016

I wrote *"A Place Called Home,"* for my friend, Kym Swank. Kym was my Vinyasa Yoga instructor in Reston, Virginia in 2014. She has made a lasting impression and inspired me to become the best version of myself. One of many poems inspired by our friendship.

"Everyday is a journey, and the journey itself is home."
~ Matsuo Basho

A PLACE CALLED HOME

The winds are howling as I walk alone,
Wrapped in my sweater, I began to roam…
As I gaze to the lights of the Northern sky,
These tears of hurt, they flood my eyes…

A cascade of memories left behind,
Nobody asked about the pain inside…
A constant struggle to be good enough,
Life-changing choices when times were tough…

I opened my wings like a mighty sparrow,
But fate shot me down with a poisoned arrow…
A temporary detour was years in the making,
It was time to go to keep my heart from aching…

Now I gaze to the lights of the Southern sky,
These specks of light, they flood my eyes…
Where the robins came to build their nests,
Bringing the spirit of hope into my chest…

My toes touch the floor, and still I rise,
These tender wounds have made me wise…
The winds are calm with nowhere to roam,
Wrapped in my sweater, *In A Place Called Home*…

Photo Credit: Laura R. Michaels © 2017

AFTER THE RAIN

When life itself is making you scared,
And you lie awake feeling unprepared...
The circles of doubt racing through your mind,
Leaving you stranded on the road behind...

Stand on the edge and don't look down,
Believe in the net before the ground...
Remember the lessons that you have learned,
Trust in yourself, so you don't get burned...

If you let your fears live in your heart,
The walls will shatter and fall apart...
So, cast your worries to the flying dove,
And leave a space for someone to love...

This give and take, will question your faith,
Only you can decide whether to run or wait...
But once you've tasted what is truly possible,
You will find your way around any obstacle...

So, follow the rainbow and see the gold,
Something new is bound to unfold...
Life will change, but it doesn't mean pain,
The clouds go home, soon *After the Rain*...

GRATITUDE

"Enjoy the little things, for one day you may look back and realize they were the big things."
~ R. Brault

"Stop acting as if life is a rehearsal. Live this day as if it were your last. The past is over and gone. The future is not guaranteed."
~ Wayne Dyer

A RUNAWAY HORSE

This is a poem that is specific to time,
Not just a story that is meant to rhyme…
Time is a continuum that we all share,
The same ear listens when we say a prayer…

Life begins with the sun in our eyes,
Growing stronger and taller toward the light…
But we never think that it is the same sun,
The one still shining when our life is done…

Like watching a movie for the second time,
You can't change the script by pressing rewind…
Like a time-lapse bud that blooms to a flower,
Seconds become minutes that turn into hours…

The eroding nature of time is always there,
Whether you are here, there, or anywhere…
One day you're teaching your baby to talk,
And before you know it, they help you to walk…

Thoughts are like roommates inside of your head,
So live with the ones that will serve you best…
Be in the present moment without remorse,
Before time escapes like *A Runaway Horse*…

"Every man goes down to his death bearing in his hands only that which he has given away."
~ Persian Proverb

ONE BREATH AWAY

Be open to what life is offering you,
And be in the moment in all that you do…
We all have a gift that we're meant to share,
As you walk your journey become aware…

There are so many lessons still to learn,
Stop repeating the pattern and make the turn…
If you know what you feel but not what you say,
Then share your love and don't waste the day…

Believe that life is rigged in your favor,
And stay the course and never waiver…
Younger eyes are looking up at you,
While older eyes are guiding you too…

Dance to the beat of your own drum,
And let kind words roll from your tongue…
Sync your heart to the rhythm of your soul,
Then your musical score will never grow old…

Life is measured by the love that you gave,
It's not your résumé that gets read by the grave…
Now count your blessings and seize the day,
And remember that death is only *One Breath Away*…

Photo Credit: Laura R. Michaels © 2017

IN OUR CREATOR'S EYE

Find gratitude that you are alive today,
Know that *God* is with you all the way...
Allow the extra time as you lie awake,
And approach this day with amazing grace...

Notice the sky whether it's cloudy or blue,
The sun will rise on the dark side of the moon...
Darkness has an intention that we may not see,
Just as the buried seed can become a tree...

These lives that surround you encompass your life,
Tethered to you - may they soar like a kite...
Our days are numbered, and we never know when,
So spread love and peace and cherish your friends...

One day at a time around the sun,
It only happens once - so make it fun...
Do what you love, and your love will grow,
You never know which way the wind will blow...

Like magical fireflies that swarm in the night,
May the light in your heart be shining bright...
Find your beacon of hope in the evening sky,
You are the reflection *In Our Creator's Eye*...

Photo Credit: Laura R. Michaels © 2017

LEARN TO FORGIVE

We've all known someone that loved to dance,
And we've all had to "let it go" and take a chance…
We've all sang in harmony to our favorite song,
And we've all hoped that angels were singing along…

We've all listened to stories that felt like our own,
And we've all walked down a road we've never known…
We've all tasted a sweetness that stole our breath,
And we've all taken risks when there was nothing left…

We've all seen someone that caught our eye,
And we've all loved someone that made us lie…
We've all known someone with a familiar soul,
And we've all needed a friend with a hand to hold…

We've all had someone that we've loved and lost,
And we've all had someone whose path we crossed…
We've all known someone that struggles with life,
And we've all fallen to our knees when we heard they died…

We've all had someone that put the beat in our heart,
And we've all had someone that gave us a new start…
We've all been given a purpose and a reason to live,
And we all taste freedom when we *Learn to Forgive*…

"Be kind whenever possible and it's always possible."
~ Dalai Lama

SOWING THE SEEDS

You woke up this morning with a brand new chance,
To help someone smile with your charming glance...
Visit the lonely and show them you care,
It's so important to make time to spare...

Never underestimate the impact you have,
Your beautiful eyes can make someone glad...
Tip the ones that serve you today,
They need the means to go out and play...

Be kind and gentle with the aging ones,
Do what you can to help them have fun...
Be patient when they shuffle at a slower pace,
They've already battled life's crazy race...

Find compassion for the mother who calms her child,
She spends most of her day taming the wild...
She's accomplished so much to make it out the door,
Criss-crossing around the toys on the floor...

Take the time to recognize the family provider,
For they carry the load so hug them tighter...
Open your eyes to see another's needs,
And spend your life, *Sowing the Seeds*...

"Develop an attitude of gratitude, and give thanks for everything that happens to you, knowing that every step forward is a step toward achieving something bigger and better than your current situation."
~ B. Tracy

WHAT YOU ALREADY HAVE

There are times in life when we feel so bummed,
And the world around us is comfortably numb…
We rise each day with a steady routine,
Nothing to expect but the same old scene…

We look in the mirror at the lines on our face,
A daily reminder of the time that we waste…
We lose the passion in the familiar touch,
And neglect the lives that mean so much…

We run around in the same old wheel,
Reaching our goal and closing the deal…
Checking the boxes of our daily lists,
Another day gone from those we miss…

Full speed ahead and eyes on the road,
There is so much to do to carry this load…
Look over there, their lives look great!
They must be happy going out on a date…

But, things aren't always what they seem,
The fear is in our mind of what we perceive…
So, don't lie awake at night and feel so sad,
You need to love *What You Already Have*…

THE TIMES

"Nothing ever goes away until it teaches us what we need to know."
~ Pema Chodron

Photo Credit: Getty Images: MLaden Anthonov ©2015

The White House is lightened in the rainbow colors in Washington D.C. on June 26, 2015. The US Supreme Court ruled that gay marriage is a nationwide right.

ALIGNING THE STARS

As a married gay woman in these United States,
I have lived a life surrounded by bigotry and hate...
On Friday, June Twenty-Sixth, Twenty Fifteen,
America's same-sex marriage ruling felt like a dream...

Love between same-sexes is love all the same,
And what an honor it is to share the same name...
Some will call it a "lifestyle choice" and never understand,
That marriage is not defined between a woman and a man...

Our family tree will now include the name of my spouse,
The Marriage Certificate hangs proudly in our house...
When family born after me goes searching for their past,
They will now see our names as a member of the cast...

I no longer need to omit or deny who I am,
I can display my wedding pictures and not give a damn...
I served my country during a time when it was forbidden,
And now I am so proud of our gay servicemen and women...

Should I lie in the hospital in search of my wife,
She can sit beside me during my pain and strife...
And when I die, the state can't take what is rightfully hers,
She can have it all, because it's what she deserves...

Since my very first paycheck in my youth,
I have paid my taxes without living my truth...
Some will never know the pain of hiding who you are,
And we thank you, President Obama, for *Aligning the Stars*...

Photo credit: Adam Bouska© 2015
In photo (left to right): Sarah Madison Donnem, Laura "Dash" Michaels, River Michaels, and Michele Marquis

The NOH8 Campaign® is a photographic silent protest created by celebrity photographer Adam Bouska and partner Jeff Parshley in direct response to the passage of Proposition 8. Photos feature subjects with duct tape over their mouths, symbolizing their voices being silenced by Prop 8 and similar legislation around the world, with "NOH8" painted on one cheek in protest (www.noh8campaign.com).

I wrote this poem, *"Lost Their Pulse,"* in dedication to the 49 souls that died after being shot at Pulse, a gay nightclub in Orlando, Florida on June 12, 2016.

LOST THEIR PULSE

These thoughts that brew inside of you,
Will manifest itself in all that you do…
When you look at me with eyes of hate,
Because unlike you, I am not straight…

When you loaded the bullets, what did you think?
Did you strap on your vest and not even blink?
When you got in your car to drive to the club,
Did you think that you could kill the love?

In the middle of this poem, they are still alive,
They are dancing to the beat with hearts open wide…
A Snap Chat video and sending tweets to the sky,
They have no idea they are about to die…

Now forty-nine souls have died in vain,
Because of the hate that ran through your veins…
The grieving is unbearable for those left behind,
A crime so heinous, they are out of their minds…

A mother will pick up her phone expecting a text,
But it's never going to come, so what happens next?
What you believed as your truth was nothing but false,
And now so many loved ones have *Lost Their Pulse*…

Photo Credit: Linda Spillers/Associated Press ©2001

"The Angelic Voice," tells the true story of a Pentagon K-9 Police Officer, Isaac Ho'opi'i, and his response and recovery efforts on September 11, 2001. Ho'opi'i was one of the first on the scene after the terrorist attack on the Pentagon and was instrumental in helping the injured and saving lives. He was awarded the *"Secretary Medal of Valor,"* and was most recently recognized again by the President of the United States on September 11, 2017.

I first met Isaac, in 1999, when he was a student in my computer training class at the Pentagon. As a native Hawaiian, Isaac embodies the true "Aloha" loving spirit. This poem is for you, my friend.

Isaac Ho'opi'i appears in this book on page 77, a reminder of the flight number of American Airlines Flight 77 that flew into the Pentagon.

THE ANGELIC VOICE

It is not every day that a hero is born,
When lives are broken and hearts are torn...
He heard on the radio when the terrorist attacked,
When the Twin Towers suffered the impact...

Suddenly, a hijacked plane zooms overhead,
The innocent passengers would soon be dead....
He ran into the building to take a chance,
As the Pentagon flames began to dance...

The smoke was thick as he fell to the floor,
He talked many people to the light of the door...
"If you can hear me now, walk towards my voice,"
To enter the building, was his only choice...

With each new cry that led to a person,
Were many more whose condition has worsened...
Back and forth, he ran down the corridor,
With every trip, there was endless horror...

Haunted with grief because he couldn't save more,
The echoes of the innocent, he can never ignore...
But for those that lived, they can all rejoice,
And be grateful for the man, with *The Angelic Voice*...

Photo credit: M.E.I.N. ©2017

Melissa Etheridge has been the most influential singer, songwriter, musician that has affected my life most powerfully. It is her music I play when I am feeling broken, and the same is true for when I am flying high. This photo is one of several "meet and greets" I have done with her, but this one was special. It was my 50th birthday, and she sang *"Mercy"* (from her album, "Lucky" 2004) at my request during sound check that blew my mind! That song got me through the toughest times in my life. It was a manifestation of a dream I had imagined ten years prior that I would one day tell her what that song meant to me. The fact that she sang it for me far exceeded any expectations I could have ever imagined. In this photo, I am about to tell her how much she means and how much that song means to me. Melissa is the "real deal" with the most calming energy and authentic soul you could ever hope for in meeting a celebrity.

LOVE IN YOUR VOICE

Throughout history, there has been a rebel cause,
They held the hands of time for a momentous pause...
The ones who were different found a way,
To muster the courage of truth and seize the day...

A preponderance of people will go with the flow,
Never to question absurdity if they even know...
Like the determined salmon that swims upstream,
In the uncharted waters, you will find your dream...

There is a river of red running through our veins,
And we all beg for mercy through excruciating pain...
Like the hammer to steel that builds the shield,
Not a soul wants a love that they must conceal...

If you don't understand why another person hates,
We are not privy to the scripts of their fate...
Like the many chakras that flow through our being,
Dissolving judgment of others can be so freeing...

Like the harmonic tones from the singing bowl,
Who are we to question another man's soul...
We may never accept another person's choice,
Let the love in your heart, be the *Love in Your Voice*...

"Faith means living with uncertainty - feeling your way through life, letting your heart guide you like a lantern in the dark."
~ D. Millman

WAKE OF AN EAGLE

I saw the dress; with stripes of gold and white,
You saw the dress; with black and blue stripes…
How can we be looking at the very same dress?
When you believe it's NO, and I believe it's YES…

It is times like these when we become blind,
Staring at the same thing, it's a hoax of the mind…
Your perspective will never be the same as mine,
It's the root of many wars throughout all time…

It takes a peacemaker to bridge the gap,
When red versus blue divides our map…
You can be small and fierce like a mighty sparrow,
Or be the giant that fires the poisonous arrows…

Let us not forget the power of our words,
They spread like the wind on the wings of a bird…
They can yell and scream like a murder of crows,
Whoever shouts the loudest will steal the show…

United we stand, divided we fall,
We are the greatest nation of them all…
But we must stand together to be regal,
We all are riding in the *Wake of an Eagle*…

River Michaels

July 25, 2016

"Once the game is over, the king and the pawn go back in the same box..."
~ Anonymous

STRIKE OF A SPARK

Like a prevailing villain in a nursery rhyme,
Lives an evil force that wants control of the times…
With an army of myrmidons and a pin-up spouse,
There is a sea of red in every seat of the house…

His grip of intolerance now holds the sword,
Hiding behind the name of the *Almighty Lord*…
This amber of evil has risen to the world's stage,
And yes, it happened on the clearest of days…

There will always be a cycle of good and evil,
Until Lucifer's wings get caught in the steeple…
More lightning will strike, and more clouds will burst,
Before the devil's last ride in his lonely hearse…

There is no rainbow in the eye of the storm,
When you witness hate in its ugliest form…
We must stand in the rain until the drops are gone,
And believe in the dark there will come a dawn…

Love will win again and flow from the fountain,
And the downtrodden will stand on top of the mountain…
So, follow the light and stay out of the dark,
And remember that hope is alive in the *Strike of a Spark*…

November 11, 2016

LOVE

"Being deeply loved by someone gives you strength while loving someone deeply gives you courage."
~ Lao Tzu

"All that I am, or hope to be, I owe to my angel mother."
~ Abraham Lincoln

THIS ROAD THAT SHE PAVED

When Mother's Day rolls around this time of year,
It's not easy for the ones whose mom is not here...
There are beautiful cards in every store,
To remind you of the memories that you adore...

These are the times when you play a mental game,
Just nod to your mother and whisper her name...
These are the moments when I know she is there,
She is pushing my cart and touching my hair...

It is the smallest of things that strike a chord,
Like the sound of her laugh and so much more...
I could spot her in a crowd by the way she walked,
And my ears tuned in when I heard her talk...

It takes many years to ease this pain,
It's a pain I believe that will never go away...
I am grateful for the years that we had together,
She is the beat of my heart - always and forever...

If you still have your mother, please hold her tight,
Do whatever you can and never lose sight...
Whether you place flowers in a vase or on her grave,
Thank *God* for her and *This Road That She Paved*...

I wrote *"Standing in the Middle,"* in honor of my friend and coworker, Mitra Dashtaray. One of many poems inspired by our friendship.

"Some are born great, some achieve greatness, and some have greatness thrust upon them."
~ W. Shakespeare

STANDING IN THE MIDDLE

We only see the world through our own eyes,
Our thoughts and feelings are usually kept inside...
We send out signals of love and hope to receive,
A touch of the hand that taught us to believe...

There are three hundred and sixty degrees we can see,
This circular perspective filled with *God* and peace...
Like a lighthouse beacon, you symbolize hope,
And help those around you unable to cope...

You fiercely protect the ones that you love,
While those that betray you will never rise above...
You fear the things that you cannot control,
But your loyal army will always patrol...

Your eyes are always giving you away,
As your mighty spirit seizes the day...
Your very presence can light up a room,
And when you're gone it's much too soon...

You will never know how great you are,
And you will never know the light of your star...
You will never be able to solve this riddle,
Because you are the one *Standing in the Middle*...

"Look into my eyes and hear what I'm not saying, for my eyes speak louder than my voice ever will."
~ Anonymous

THE LOOK IN THEIR EYE

Some people you meet evoke a feeling inside,
You know it right away by the look in their eye…
The crack in their heart shines a light on you,
Like a familiar soul that you already knew…

Time melts away through the hour glass,
Exchanging painful memories from our past…
Feeling shakier than the legs of a newborn foal,
The sound of their voice can soothe your soul…

The days become weeks and over again,
Realizing now you have found a new friend…
Like the cosmic dust from a shooting star,
You can recognize just how special they are…

But when boundaries are crossed that divide the line,
Then you must decide if they are worth your time…
It seems the ones that you love cause the most pain,
When they make the choice to just walk away…

But there are some souls that you just can't let go,
As if divine intervention is forcing you to grow…
These are the ones that evoke a feeling inside,
And you knew it right away by *The Look in Their Eye*…

*"Making me feel like you want me badly is one of the sexiest, most flattering
things you can do to me."*
~ Anonymous

LIGHT THE STARS

I recognize that look in your eyes,
No need to bother with your disguise…
This energy field is a magnetic ring,
Pulling us in with a tethered string…

The spell is cast inside of my head,
Placing thoughts of us lying in bed…
Many romantic notions are hard to hide,
My shirt is open, please step inside…

Your picture breathes inside of my phone,
Rousing thoughts of you when I am alone…
And before I know it, the time has flown,
The alarm goes off and it's time to go…

I laugh and smile when I think of you,
Your clothes on the floor and your sexy shoes…
I love the way you are making me feel,
And it doesn't seem to matter if it is real…

It is the situation that creates the scene,
And the reasons why I live in your dreams…
But around the world or wherever you are,
Your kiss on my lips will *Light the Stars*…

"Because there's nothing more beautiful than the way the ocean refuses to stop kissing the shoreline, no matter how many times it's sent away."
~ Sarah Kay, No Matter the Wreckage

AWAY FROM THE SHORE

This beach-worn glass that I rub in my hand,
Is years in the making from the relentless sand...
These crashing waves that come ashore,
Still chase the ocean thirsty for more...

This water dances with a reckless joy,
Tossing seashells around like little toys...
There is an ebb and flow to our lives,
A time to coast, and a time to fly...

There are moments in life to be still,
Sometimes a mountain is merely a hill...
Love will die in a hopeless projection,
The answer lies in our reflection...

So, let the music play inside of your head,
There is peace in the words already said...
They say letting go will set you free,
The connection exists, so let it be...

Enjoy the ones that soothe your soul,
And it doesn't matter who's in control...
Someone will always be loving you more,
They live in the now, *Away from the Shore*...

Photo Credit: Maria Thackston © 2014

I KNEW IT WAS YOU

We go through life one day at a time,
With our eyes always searching for a sign…
I used to wonder why the ocean is so blue,
Then I looked to the sky, and I thought it was you…

These snow-capped mountains that rise so high,
So majestic and jagged and touch the sky…
I used to wonder how long a bird could swoon,
Then I felt the wind, and I thought it was you…

I love the evening sky with a big bright moon,
And how it lights the way when it's over too soon…
I used to wonder how the waves could be in tune,
Then I looked to the shore, and I thought it was you…

After all this time, the morning light still appears,
How it eases the pain after a night filled with tears…
I used to wonder why the grass bathes in dew,
Then I felt the earth, and I thought it was you…

This heart pumps blood that runs through my veins,
And it keeps me alive even when I'm filled with pain…
I used to wonder why my heart always stayed true,
Then I looked inside, and *I Knew It Was You*…

SELF-REFLECTION

"If I have harmed anyone in any way either knowingly or unknowingly through my own confusions, I ask their forgiveness.

If anyone has harmed me in any way either knowingly or unknowingly through their own confusions, I forgive them.

And if there is a situation I am not yet ready to forgive, I forgive myself for that.

For all the ways that I harm myself, negate, doubt, belittle myself, judge or be unkind to myself through my own confusions, I forgive myself."

~ Buddhist Wisdom

"After being with you, no one can tell me that I haven't touched the stars."
~ A. Asher

AMONG THE STARS

At times, there is a void deep inside,
My very own real estate with a key to hide…
It's a place that I visit when I'm feeling blue,
Where I fall to my knees on an imagined pew…

This is where I go to evaluate things,
Where I give it life, or I give it wings….
Many broken stairs lead to this room,
Where my love will die, or it will bloom…

It's a place to go when I cry till dawn,
Crawling through memories of what is gone…
When my heart is yearning for what I miss,
It is a place to go and reminisce…

This is not a place where I stay too long,
It's where the piano plays the saddest song…
There's a gracious line between light and dark,
Where these tender thoughts carry a spark…

Now I have created a space with a skylight view,
Where the Galaxy dances in the midnight blue…
It's a place with sounds from a sweet guitar,
Where I count myself *Among the Stars*…

Photo Credit: River Michaels © 2017
Painting by: Lori Anne Boocks

A DIFFERENT SEA

As I travel along this journey of mine,
I see blips of light in the souls that shine...
Like a needle that's guided by the radio dial,
I know when it's time for me to stay awhile...

I have pondered what lies behind their eyes,
Unknowing teachers have made me wise...
Some of these scholars have paralyzed me,
And the ones I needed let me be...

My hand extends to the wounded sparrow,
The one who bleeds from the poison arrow...
The answers have always been in front of my face,
When I gave from my heart, I was touching grace...

With love and compassion as my guiding force,
I have wrestled the reins of the restless horse...
Even the wildest steed will eventually break,
And the pain is gone when they finally wake...

With freedom to ride into the western sky,
I am counting the stars as I say goodbye...
I may not be who you want me to be,
I am the River that pours into *A Different Sea*...

*"No man ever steps in the same river twice, for it's not the same river and he's
not the same man."*
~ Heraclitus

SAME RIVER TWICE

Your footsteps will always follow you around,
And your shadow will always be on the ground...
But without the light the shadow is blind,
It is life and death at the same time...

The cherry blossoms bloom for just a few days,
Then the wind comes along and blows them away...
Their beauty is extraordinary and so short lived,
A reminder of impermanence is what they give...

If you have a dream, you should live it now,
Before the curtain falls and you take a bow...
Listen to the voice that calls your name,
Awaken yourself to never be the same...

Open your heart and let love flow,
Believe in the seeds covered in snow...
Spring will come and give them life,
Knowing the sun will rise after the night...

Recognize love in its various forms,
And the beauty that lives in a majestic storm...
Swim in the waters that feel so nice,
You will never step in the *Same River Twice*...

"How far you go in life depends on your being tender with the young, compassionate with the aged, sympathetic with the striving and tolerant of the weak and strong. Because someday in your life you will have been all of these."
~ G. W. Carver

BOTH YOUNG AND OLD

Everyone we meet, we show a different side,
To some, we show it all, and to others we hide...
A song can spark a mood to change who we are,
And light up the dust in each of our stars...

These lines of history and all their companions,
Striping the walls of the mighty Grand Canyon...
So much life before us and so much yet to be,
Or has it already happened and we just can't see?

Life is an endless lesson in love and loss,
Before and after the *Man* on the cross...
Time is a poison when love has flown,
It's also the reason that you have grown...

I will never love enough in my time,
Despite the sting of a painful goodbye...
I believe I can be whomever I choose,
Walking this world in my travelin' shoes...

To answer your question, who am I?
I live my life just being kind...
I paint these words to reflect my soul,
Of who I am, *Both Young and Old*...

Photo Credit: Laura R. Michaels ©2017

"With strong, new wings for her security,
   the spirit of a butterfly has been set free...
Spreading peace and joy for all who see,
   her passion for life thru her poetry...
With strong, new wings and ready to fly,
   this delicate soul paints the perfect sky...
Like an artist who waits for a canvas to dry,
   by smelling the fumes that caught your eye...
With strong, new wings and feeling grand,
   the beautiful butterfly now can stand...
As she buries her feet down into the sand,
   a treasure is held in the palm of her hand...
With strong, new wings full of emotion,
   she's testing the waters for love and devotion...
Like slow, steady waves found in a calm ocean,
   look deep down inside for the river in motion..."
~ Laura R. Michaels

"What you think, you become. What you feel, you attract. What you imagine, you create.
~ Buddha

I AM RIVER

When I stare at the mountain and its beautiful form,
I reflect on the good and then I ponder the storms…
There are days when I wish that I could touch the sky,
And right all the wrongs and to answer the whys…

When people from your past still think you're the same,
But everything is different but the memory of your name…
We live in the thoughts of those who have crossed our paths,
Some we have hurt, and in others, we have laughed…

We may never know why we must go through pain,
But for every heartache, we add a link to the chain…
As a heliocentric being that has done many laps,
I find myself wanting to fill in the gaps…

As a metaphor of the mountain in its majesty,
I see the sum of our hearts that live in our families…
And for every jagged edge that our lives have carved,
It represents times of abundance and the times we've starved…

If today feels like a replica of a mundane yesterday,
Remember that you are one mile further down life's highway…
So, in a world full of takers, it is more fun to be a giver,
And if you ever need a friend, know that *I Am River*…

About the Author

Photo Credit: Laura R. Michaels ©2017

Award-winning American Poet, River C. Michaels served as an Aviation Electrician's Mate and one of the first female Naval Aircrewman in the United States Navy. Following her naval career, she became a government contractor and served as an Information Technology instructor at the Pentagon during the September 11, 2001 terrorist attack timeframe. As fate would have it on that Tuesday morning, she was safe at home.

Michaels is pursuing her Doctor of Philosophy from the University of the Rockies. She has a Master of Arts degree from Webster University in Computer Resources and Information Systems, and a Bachelor of Science degree from Southern Illinois University at Carbondale in Education, Training and Development.

The strongest and most inspirational influence in River's life has always been and continues to be, her late mother who died in September 2001. For more information, or to contact the author, please send your email to: River@RiverMichaels.com

I AM

I am not I.
I am this one
walking beside me whom I do not see,
whom at times I manage to visit,
and whom at other times I forget;
who remains calm and silent while I talk,
and forgives, gently, when I hate,
who walks where I am not,
who will remain standing when I die.

~ Juan Ramón Jiménez

Other Books by River Michaels

Forever Spoken © 2007 by the International Library of Poetry as a compilation. Includes the award-winning poem, *"Red Velvet Dragonfly."*

Michaels, R. M. (2008). *A River of Rain - Book of Poetry*. Denver, Colorado: Outskirts Press. ISBN: 978-1-4327-2224-1, Library of Congress Control Number: 2008923717.

Michaels, R. M. (2009). *A River of Peace - Book of Poetry*. Denver, Colorado: Outskirts Press. ISBN: 978-1-4327-4191-4, Library of Congress Control Number: 2009929293.

Michaels, R. M. (2013). *Pure River - Book of Poetry*. Clifton, Virginia: Lulu. ISBN: 978-0-578-12650-0.